SALT LAKE COUNTY LIBRARY SYSTEM
purchased at Public Sale

Ancestor Hunting

JULIAN MESSNER NEW YORK

Ancestor Hunting

by Lorraine Henriod

Illustrated by Janet Potter D'Amato

Copyright © 1979 by Lorraine Henriod
Illustrations Copyright © 1979 by Janet Potter D'Amato

All rights reserved including the right of reproduction in whole or in part in any form. Published by Julian Messner, a Simon & Schuster Division of Gulf & Western Corporation, Simon & Schuster Building, 1230 Avenue of the Americas, New York, N.Y. 10020.

Manufactured in the United States of America

Design by Alex D'Amato

Library of Congress Cataloging in Publication Data

Henriod, Lorraine.
  Ancestor hunting.

  Includes index.
  SUMMARY: A guide to finding information about one's ancestors.
  1. Genealogy—Juvenile literature. [1. Genealogy] I. D'Amato, Janet. II. Title.
CS15.5.H46   929'.1   79-10767
ISBN 0-671-32998-7

Contents

CHAPTER

1

You Are Special   7

2

Ancestor Hunting in the Past   13

3

Beginning Your Ancestor Hunt   22

4

Working on Your Charts   30

5

Hunting for Grandparents
 and Great-grandparents   38

6

Completing Your Family History   52

7

Some Special Projects   56

Glossary   63

Index   64

You Are Special

Do you know anybody in the whole world who looks exactly like you? Who thinks the thoughts you do? Who likes to do the same things you like to do? Of course not.

There isn't any person in this world who is just like you. Even an identical twin will deny being just like the other twin.

What makes you the way you are? Partly, qualities you inherited from your parents and grandparents and all your other ancestors. You and all the other people of your *generation* have a tremendous number of ancestors.

Your generation means the people who were born at about the same time you were. Your parents belong to another generation. Your grandparents are part of still another generation. One generation lasts about thirty years. When you look back six generations, you have 126 ancestors. That is about 180-200 years.

Perhaps you look like your father or mother or have some features of each of them. Perhaps you look like one of your grandparents or great-grandparents. Or somebody farther back. That's almost hard to believe, isn't it? In spite of the fact that a relative may be a complete stranger to you, he or she helped make you the individual you are.

Heredity, the passing of characteristics from generation to generation, has given you a lot more than just your looks. It may have given you a tendency to be good at singing or drawing or math. But this tendency is only a chance to be talented. It is not a promise that you will be good at anything. It will not help you unless you develop it by study and practice.

All by itself, heredity is not responsible for the person you are. Your *environment*, the place where you live and the opportunities that are part of your everyday life, also had a lot to do with your becoming the person you are. Perhaps you are a good horseback rider. You may be lucky enough to live on a ranch, and have a chance to do a lot of riding. If you lived in a city, you might not be as good a rider. You could still have the natural ability but perhaps you would not have an opportunity to ride at all. Without practice, that inborn ability could not grow.

If you are good at astronomy, maybe you should give part of the credit to some scientific ancestor. And, of course, part is due to the fact that you live near a fine planetarium. In your case, like that of the horseback rider, heredity and environment worked together.

Even without natural ability, a person can learn to do almost anything with plenty of practice. To become an expert, you need both a natural gift and a good environment, plus a willingness to work very hard at developing the gift. You can change your environment, but your heredity was decided before you were born.

Since they are so important in your life, would you like to become acquainted with the people in your family who helped you become such a special you?

It would be great if you had some kind of machine that could take you backward in time. Then you could meet your ancestors face to face. Since that kind of machine does not exist, you will have to be a detective, hunting down clues until you find out about your ancestors. This kind of detective work means you will be trying to find your *roots* so that you will know more about yourself.

You won't need fancy equipment for your ancestor hunt. All you will need is a notebook, a large manila envelope, a pencil and, most important, a lot of curiosity.

For many people, ancestor hunting is an interesting hobby. For others, the search becomes too important to be called a hobby.

Back in 1970, a Russian sailor jumped overboard and tried to swim to shore when his fishing vessel came close to the United States. He was picked up by the Coast Guard, who made him go back to his ship after his captain demanded his return.

The story of Simas Kudrika, who tried to escape to freedom, appeared in most American newspapers the next day. He had lived in Lithuania when that country was taken over by the Russians during World War II. He didn't think of himself as a Russian.

Lithuanian-Americans took up his case, a case that seemed hopeless. Some of them thought they remembered a woman who had gone back to

Lithuania after her birth in the United States. They recalled that later she had married a man whose name was Kudrika.

The Lithuanian-Americans tried to get help from the Kudrikas in Russia, but were not successful. However, they were experienced ancestor-hunters. They followed clues and found the mother's birth record in Brooklyn, N.Y.

Four years after Simas Kudrika tried to escape from a Russian fishing vessel, he came back to the United States with his wife, son, daughter and mother. His mother was already a United States citizen. Now citizenship was possible for the rest of the family because of some stubborn ancestor-hunters who would not give up.

Even if your story is not as dramatic as the Kudrikas', it will be more interesting to you. After all, it will be *your* story.

Ancestor Hunting in the Past

All over the United States—all over the world, in fact—people, young and old, are tracking down clues as part of the fast-growing hobby, *genealogy*, or ancestor hunting. For the last hundred years, genealogy has been considered an international science. In the last ten years, it has taken on new life.

It all began with the ancient people who were able to keep track of family history even though they did not know how to write. They used what we call the oral tradition. The ancient people recited poetry and sang songs as they gathered around their campfires. Many of these poems and songs told about their families.

The custom of memorizing family histories

continued in some places. The Maoris of New Zealand, for instance, were trained to recite their family lines back to the time when their people migrated to that land, in about the fourteenth century, A.D. For many years, the Incas in Peru and the Hebrews could repeat their genealogies from memory.

Even today in Africa, each tribe has a man who can recite the history of all the families in the village. He is called a *griot*. When one griot dies, the history is not lost. Another man has been trained to take his place.

Maori storyteller.

Tribal griot.

As soon as writing was invented, the histories of the kings who ruled were carved into stone. Finally, *papyrus* and then *parchment* made it easier to write things down. These are two early kinds of writing paper. Now kings weren't the only subjects of stories. Gods and goddesses were, too.

The ancient Greeks and Romans believed in gods and goddesses. Their religion taught that certain families could be traced back to them.

Many Greeks kept records, trying to prove they were related to gods and goddesses. Romans who belonged to the nobility wrote genealogies to show that they were not of the common people, but were also related to kings or gods.

The Hebrews were especially interested in family history. The Old Testament contains pages of genealogy, which traced Biblical families back to the beginning of history.

During the Middle Ages, the nobility in Europe kept track of their ancestors for a very good reason. Only men who could prove they belonged to the nobility could become knights. Starting in the twelfth century, the knights had special markings on their shields which showed what family the knights

Knight in armor.

belonged to. And if the family was that of a king, the markings would show it. The markings were passed from father to son. This custom is called *heraldry*.

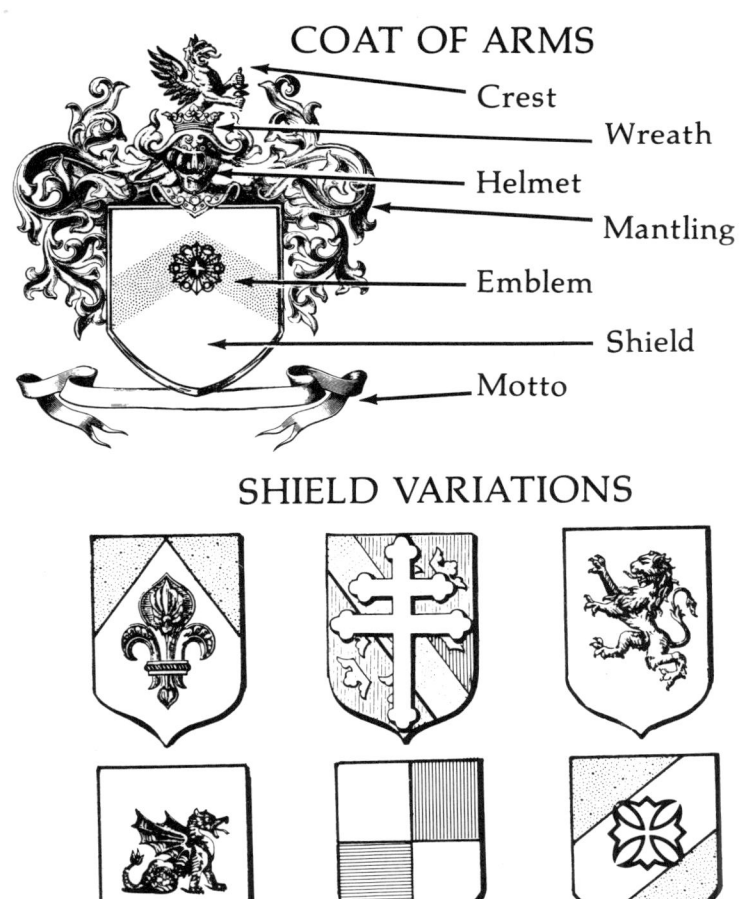

A knight carried a shield which showed either his own coat of arms or that of his family. The crest might be an animal or object. The shield had many variations. It could display designs, animals, birds (real or imaginary), flowers or symbols. Each had a special meaning.

The Mayflower.

Genealogy has always been popular in the United States. Many Americans traced their ancestors back to the first settlers, especially those who came aboard the *Mayflower*. But in 1976, two separate events pushed genealogy into first place among American hobbies. That year was the two-hundredth birthday of the United States. Lots of people became interested in history, generally, and their own family history, most of all.

The second event was even more responsible for the growing interest in genealogy. It was the publication of a book called *Roots* by Alex Haley. The author was able to trace his ancestors back through slavery in this country to their beginnings in Africa. He had asked "Who am I?" and had found an answer. The book was later made into a television show, and more people watched it than had ever watched any tv program before.

Mr. Haley tells everybody that his famous ancestor hunt would have been easier if he had started his search for his roots when he was a boy. In his book, he describes himself when he was very young, sitting on the front porch of his grandmother's home in Tennessee. His grandmother and her sisters sat on the porch by the hour, rocking and repeating stories their grandparents had told them.

He wasn't interested in ancestor hunting until many of the ladies, who had sat on that porch and rocked and talked, had died. He hadn't written down the stories they told each other. This made the search much harder. Years later, he tried to remember every word they had said. Only one elderly cousin remained to help him as he hunted for his roots.

Mr. Haley believes people come closer to understanding each other when they really understand themselves. He says that if everyone will develop an interest in his own roots, he or she will come to have respect for the beginnings of other people. That way the world will come closer to peace.

Many people started searching for their roots. The Boy Scouts of America added a merit badge on genealogy. Workers in genealogical libraries became accustomed to seeing young people.

In September 1978, a very special kind of genealogical library was opened at Doraville, near Atlanta, Georgia. It was designed to be used by everyone, including those in wheelchairs and the blind and deaf. Ramps and railings were added in many places so that people in wheelchairs could move about in the building. For the blind, records are in Braille and on tape. To assist deaf patrons, volunteers have learned sign language.

The largest genealogical library in the world is in Salt Lake City, Utah. It is the Genealogical Library of the Church of Jesus Christ of Latter-day Saints, better known as the Mormon Church.

This library is part of the Genealogical Society of Utah. Money for its operation comes from the Mormon Church. Probably some members of your family are named on the nearly one million rolls of microfilm there. Each month, thousands more are added!

Workers at this library do not do research for ancestor hunters, but they are there to help people who come to the library. This service is free of charge. More than 280 branch libraries have been started in many parts of the world and they are free, too. Fifty more branches begin operation each year.

Why are the Mormons so interested in ancestor hunting? Their religion teaches that families are forever, that they are not broken up by death. Mormons hunt for their ancestors so the whole family can be together in the next life.

Are you curious about your roots? Curious enough to go ancestor hunting, looking for names of the people who came before you in your own family? You will find the dates when they lived and, most important of all, their stories.

The Genealogical Library of the Church of Jesus Christ of Latter-day Saints.

Beginning Your Ancestor Hunt

Your genealogy hobby has two parts. First, you write your life story, answering the questions your children and grandchildren would probably ask. Second, you hunt for your ancestors.

How do you start? Imagine the questions a stranger from another country—better still, another planet—would ask you. Try to wonder about yourself, the way a Martian might. Now let the questions fly.

"Do you go to school? What are you studying? What does your school look like?"

"Do you live in a big city? In the country?"

"Describe the place where you live. How many other people live there?"

Answer these questions, and you will be off to a good start on your life story.

Have you ever had a "pen pal?" Has someone you know ever had one? Sometimes a school teacher gives to her students the names of children in other countries who want to write to an American their own age. Telling a pen pal all about yourself is a lot like writing your own story.

Your pen pal, children and grandchildren will want to know what you look like. Are you tall? Or are you small for your age and always hoping to grow tall? Do you like sports, and what are your favorite ones? They will be curious about your home life. Do you have any brothers or sisters? Does your family like to do things together? Do they argue a lot? What is your favorite food? Tell about your interests, as well as your dreams, your likes and your dislikes.

As soon as you begin writing your own story, you have started the record of your family. When

your story is complete—up to the very day you finish writing—it will be time to start getting acquainted with some of the other people who helped make you such a special person.

In this ancestor-hunting project, you will get acquainted with the 14 people who came before you in your family—your two parents, your four grandparents and your eight great-grandparents.

The first step is to start searching for the names and dates—birth, marriage, and death dates of all these people. You will also need to know the places where they were born, married and died. Don't be surprised when you have to ask aunts, uncles, cousins, even family friends, to help in the search.

Unfortunately, your ancestors didn't leave autobiographies to help you get to know them. It is up

to you to do all the detective work that you'll need in order to write a biography of them. A *biography* is the life story of a person written by someone else. An *autobiography* is the life story written by the person who lived it.

You can solve this problem for your *descendants*, the people who come after you in your family, by using the "5 w's." Newspaper reporters, who sometimes have to be like detectives, use the "5 w's" in writing their stories. You will need to know who, what, where, when and why. In ancestor hunting, these words are used to find out as much as possible: who the ancestors were, what they did, where they lived, when they lived, and why you need to know about them.

All of this information must be recorded on a pedigree chart. *Pedigree* means the line of ancestors of a person or an animal. Because one generation follows another, we can use the word "line." A pedigree chart is a way of recording your ancestors by generation. Your pedigree chart will show your family tree. Your ancestors are your roots.

You can buy a blank pedigree chart or you can easily make your own, as in the drawing. The first column will contain your name and those of your parents. The second column will be for your grandparents, and the third for your great-grandparents.

Your immediate ancestors are your parents, grandparents and great-grandparents—fourteen, count them!

PEDIGREE CHART

PARENTS YOUR GRANDPARENTS

Name _____
Born _____
Married _____
Died _____

YOUR FATHER

Name _____
Born _____
Married _____
Died _____

FATHER'S FATHER

FATHER'S MOTHER

Name _____
Born _____
Married _____
Died _____

YOU!

Name _____
Born _____
Place _____

MOTHER'S FATHER

Name _____
Born _____
Married _____
Died _____

YOUR MOTHER

Name _____
Born _____
Married _____
Died _____

MOTHER'S MOTHER

Name _____
Born _____
Married _____
Died _____

PEDIGREE CHART (cont.)

YOUR GREAT-GRANDPARENTS

Name _____
Born _____ Place _____ Married _____ Place _____
Died _____ Place _____

Name _____
Born _____ Place _____ Married _____
Died _____ Place _____

Name _____
Born _____ Place _____ Married _____ Place _____
Died _____ Place _____

Name _____
Born _____ Place _____ Married _____
Died _____ Place _____

Name _____
Born _____ Place _____ Married _____ Place _____
Died _____ Place _____

Name _____
Born _____ Place _____ Married _____
Died _____ Place _____

Name _____
Born _____ Place _____ Married _____ Place _____
Died _____ Place _____

Name _____
Born _____ Place _____ Married _____
Died _____ Place _____

Next, you can make a family group sheet for each couple. That makes seven family group sheets. This sheet will list all of one couple's (your parents, for instance) children along with their birth, marriage and death dates. As you hunt for names for your pedigree chart, some other names are bound to turn up. These will be your aunts, uncles and cousins.

FAMILY GROUP

Husband's Name _____
MARRIED TO
Wife's Maiden Name _____

Date _____ Place _____

HUSBAND _____
    Born _____ Place _____
    Died _____ Place _____
    Occupation _____
    Father's Full Name _____
    Mother's Full Maiden Name _____

WIFE _____
    Born _____ Place _____
    Died _____ Place _____
    Occupation _____
    Father's Full Name _____
    Mother's Full Maiden Name _____

Other Marriages _____

FAMILY GROUP

CHILDREN OF

_____ & _____
Husband's Name   Wife's Maiden Name

*Child's Name	Date Born	Place	M** or F	Married	Died

Additional Information _____

_____

_____

_____

  * List each child (whether living or dead) in order of birth. To indicate that a child is an ancestor of the family representative, place an X next to the name.
** Indicate whether child is male (M) or (F)

Working on Your Charts

Now that you have started to write your own story, you are forging, or making, the first link in the chain that is your family history. You can begin work on the chain at home.

Before your mother goes food shopping, she checks the refrigerator and cupboards to see what she needs. In a way, you will do the same thing. Only you will be checking with the people at home to see what information they have.

You already have the pedigree chart and the family group sheets. Besides those forms, you will need:

A pencil.

A loose-leaf notebook that uses 8½" × 11" lined paper.

A manila envelope the size of your notebook.

Fasten the envelope with scotch tape to the inside of the back cover of your notebook. Put your pedigree chart, the family group sheets, and any letters or pictures you will be collecting inside the envelope.

Sometimes you may not have your notebook with you when you have a chance to take notes. Don't try to memorize these facts. Write the information on any kind of paper you can get. Later, when you're at home, copy it into the notebook.

Ask the members of your family to help you fill in the chart. Probably all the spaces won't be filled up at first. You were planning to do some detective work, weren't you? While you are searching, don't misplace the pedigree chart. Be sure it is in the envelope whenever you aren't writing on it.

Ask your parents for the names and addresses of any relatives who may be able to help. Write these down in your notebook, along with their telephone numbers, if they live near you. You will also be writing letters. Make a record in your notebook to whom you write each day. Keep the replies in the envelope.

To help you write your family history, collect pictures and put them in the envelope, too. Someone in your family may have pasted photos in an album, or kept them in a box. They may be willing to loan them to you. Take a good look at the photos. You may see in them old cars, railroad trains, furniture, signs and other objects. These will give you some idea about the people and how they lived in the past. Notice, too, their clothes and how they wore their hair.

Diplomas, *certificates* of birth, marriage or death, and newspaper clippings are also good sources of information. If your parents don't have a special place for these papers, offer to store them in your trusty envelope. As you can see, the government makes out legal papers for every big event in a person's life.

If you have a grandmother or grandfather living with your family, the pedigree chart, your notebook and the envelope will fill up faster than if you have to go somewhere else for information. They will have some wonderful stories to tell you. They also keep many objects and photos that have been handed down to them from their parents.

If your parents are divorced, and they have homes in your town, visit both places. You have inherited characteristics from both sides of your family. Nothing can change that fact, even if the two sides aren't on good terms now.

What if your mother or father—or a grandparent or great-grandparent—has been married more than once? Write the date and place of each marriage from which you are descended on your family group sheet. Then you should write the names of other husbands and wives on the other side of the chart.

These are a few of the pictures and documents you may collect in your search. Keep notes of all information available about each picture, and make duplicates if possible for your own collection.

Even though they are members of your family, they are not your ancestors.

Try to be sure that each name and date is correct. To do so, you have to prove that your information is the truth beyond any doubt. The word *prove* has a special meaning for genealogists. Sometimes they say *documented*, instead. It means the same as "proved."

You can prove your own birthdate by using your birth certificate. This "documents" your birth date. You needed that piece of paper once before, to prove how old you were when you started school. You will need it again, too, if you want to travel to other countries. It will prove that you are an American citizen, and the government will give you a passport.

Your parents can prove their marriage date by showing their marriage certificate.

If any of your relatives are buried in a nearby cemetery, your family may visit the graves at certain times during the year. If you have never gone along, tell them that you want to. The gravestones will tell you the date the person died.

On their summer vacation, the Bennett family took the time to visit a little cemetery in another state. They knew they had to drive through that state to reach the place where they were going. Mr. and Mrs. Bennett had been told that a great-great-grandmother of the children had been buried there after she died of cholera while on the way west.

All four children walked through the cemetery, checking the old-fashioned gravestones. They were looking for one that told about Sarah Bennett, age 21, who died in 1853.

"Here she is. Here's Sarah," nine-year-old Jimmy shouted from the far side of the cemetery.

The Bennetts even made a rubbing of Sarah's gravestone. They had brought the right materials with them. They had masking tape, some newsprint-like paper that they had bought in an art supply store, a large wax crayon and a whisk broom.

They brushed the stone clean. With masking tape, Jimmy fastened the paper tightly against the letters on the stone. Then the other children took turns rubbing the crayon against the paper. When they took it away from the stone, the writing was preserved on their paper.

GRAVESTONE RUBBING

After cleaning the stone, tape paper in place. Use two sheets if necessary to get all the information needed. Remove the wrapper of a large black crayon (such as a lumber marking crayon) and use its side. Holding the paper firmly, gently rub the crayon over the entire surface. If the paper shifts, the image might blur. Continue carefully rubbing over each area. Letters, numbers and design that were carved into the stone should appear white with black around them. Keep rubbing until the message is readable on the paper.

An example of a gravestone rubbing (greatly reduced).

Now that you have gone through the scrapbooks and the boxes of snapshots, as well as people's memories at your home, it's time to visit some other relatives. The homes of your grandparents will be the next good place to go. Then the homes of great-grandparents, if they live near you.

Hunting for Grandparents and Great-Grandparents

If you have grandparents in the city where you live, telephone and tell them you are studying the family history. Then ask what day and time would be good for you to come for a visit. Explain that you would like to talk about their lives. You would also like to know as much as they can remember about their own parents and grandparents. Your pedigree chart will not go as far back as your grandparents' grandparents. But if you should come across some names of even older ancestors or dates, make notes in your notebook.

If your family has a tape recorder and you have permission to use it, find out if your grandparents mind having their conversation taped. Some people are not comfortable when a tape recorder is going.

Ask if they have any pictures that you can have. If you are lucky, they may have several copies of some snapshots and will give you one. Anyway, study their old pictures, scrapbooks and diaries. If they have old diaries, you are really lucky.

A *diary* is a personal record of day-to-day events which some people keep. Some diaries have records of birth, death and marriage that cover many years of the life of the person who kept the diary.

Before you talk to your grandparents, prepare a list of questions. They probably have some interesting stories to tell, but make sure you get the answers to questions like these:

   1. What is your full name?
   2. Were you named after someone? Who?

3. Where and when were you born?
4. Where did you grow up? What schools did you attend?
5. Where did you meet your husband (or wife)?
6. When and where were you married?
7. What did your husband do for a living? Did he change jobs? Did he serve in the army?
8. Where did you live after you were married? How many different places?
9. What are the names of your children, and their dates and places of birth?
10. What hobbies and interests did you and your husband (wife) have?
11. What special family traditions and activities did your children enjoy while they were growing up?
12. What do you know about your family background? Get the names of the parents and grandparents of both your grandparents. Where did each of their families originate?

Don't be surprised if each question reminds your grandparents of some special event in their lives. You will probably find out things that happened in their childhood.

This information will go on the pedigree chart, the family group sheets, or in the family history you

PEDIGREE CHART

PARENTS

YOUR FATHER
Name STEPHENS, DAVID CLARK
Born Nov 3, 1942 Los Angeles
Married JUNE 15, 1968
Died

YOU!
Name STEPHENS, CAROL
Born July 4, 1970
Place Los Angeles, Calif

YOUR MOTHER
Name JONES, SUSAN
Born March 14, 1944 Wellsville UTAH
Married 1968
Died

YOUR GRANDPARENTS

FATHER'S FATHER
Name STEPHENS, PAUL
Born FEB 13, 1915 Idaho Falls, IDA
Married March 3, 1939
Died

FATHER'S MOTHER
Name HALL, MARY
Born JUNE 4, 1922 BURLEY, IDAHO
Married 1939
Died March 15, 1957 Los Angeles, CALIF

MOTHER'S FATHER
Name JONES, WALTER
Born Nov 5, 1912 Logan UTAH
Married March 8, 1940 Logan UTAH
Died

MOTHER'S MOTHER
Name PEAK, SARAH
Born April 14, 1921 Logan UTAH
Married 1940
Died June 26, 1949 LOGAN UTAH

PEDIGREE CHART (cont.)

YOUR GREAT-GRANDPARENTS

Name STEPHENS, HENRY
Born 1898 Place ENGLAND Married _____ Place _____
Died _____ Place ENGLAND

Name EVANS, AMY
Born 5/16/1899 Place WALES Married
Died _____ Place _____

Name HALL, HIRAM
Born _____ Place ST LOUIS Married _____ Place _____
Died _____ Place _____

Name _____ LYDIA
Born _____ Place _____ Married
Died _____ Place _____

Name JONES, WALTER
Born 1894 Place WALES Married _____ Place _____
Died _____ Place _____

Name POTTER, JEAN
Born 1/2/95 Place WALES Married
Died _____ Place _____

Name PEAK, JOHN
Born Jan 4, 1896 Place LONDON ENGLAND Married _____ Place _____
Died 5/19/'51 Place SALT LAKE CITY, UTAH

Name COLES, ETTA
Born _____ Place ENGLAND Married
Died _____ Place ENGLAND

Partially filled in pedigree chart.

are writing. Your pedigree chart would be more interesting if you had a picture to go with each name. It shouldn't be hard to get a small picture of your mother and father and one of yourself. If your grandparents don't have extra pictures to give you, maybe your parents will have some copies made of the best ones.

An inexpensive way to copy pictures is with a duplicating machine. Perhaps there is a machine you can use at your school. The public library probably has one. The place where your mother or father works may have one.

Gather up all the pictures you want to copy. Arrange them close together on a piece of typing paper. Use a single drop of rubber cement to hold each one in place. This kind of glue won't hurt the pictures, but it will keep them in the right spot for a few minutes. Make as many copies as you want.

Maybe your grandparents—or your parents—will let you borrow a birth certificate or a high school diploma or some other important paper long enough for you to copy it. These duplicated copies may not be as clear as if a professional photographer had made them. But for the low price you pay, they will be fine.

There may not be enough room in the manila envelope for these picture pages. Put them away in a drawer. You will need them to complete your family history.

Gathering information.

Another good source of facts is the family Bible. Many families have one. If it isn't at your home, perhaps your grandparents or some other relative will have it.

The Bible was often a wedding gift, and in it there are places to record important dates in the history of the new family. Traditionally, the father made these entries in a special place in the Bible, between the Old and New Testaments.

By the way, check the date the Bible was printed. That is known as the *copyright* date, and it is on the back of the title page. A copyright is a notice of

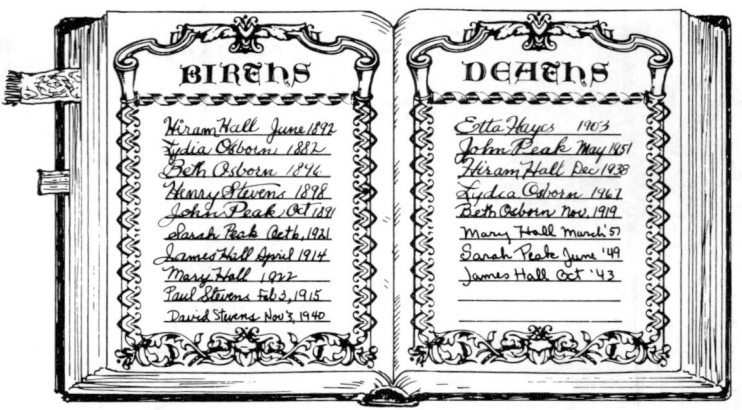

ownership of a written or printed work. Sometimes it is on the bottom of the title page. Any dates that are older than the copyright date of that particular Bible were usually written from memory long after they happened.

Many Bibles have one highly decorated page for the marriage record of the owners of the book. Blank spaces are left for the names of the couple, the date and place of marriage, name of the person who married them, and names of witnesses. Other blank pages follow. One is headed BIRTHS, another, MARRIAGES, and another, DEATHS.

If your grandparents don't live in your city, you may have to get your questions answered by mail. Or if they are ill or traveling, you may not get an answer quickly. Whenever you write someone, be sure to enclose a stamped, self-addressed envelope.

Pedigree charts are much easier to fill out if all your relatives live near you. Relatives who are far away will be glad to help, too. Just allow more time for your answers.

For instance, maybe you are the granddaughter of a man who was born in Italy. He came to the United States as a child. Your grandmother was born in this country, of Italian parents. Two great-aunts, older than your grandmother, remember living in Italy. (A great-aunt is the aunt of your mother or father.) They will be helpful in filling out family group sheets which give the names and birthdates of all your grandparents' and great-grandparents' children. Of course, these will be your aunts, uncles and cousins.

Perhaps your father says that he thinks Great-Uncle Roberto told him that your great-grandfather was born November 3, 1902, in Italy. Since your father isn't sure of his facts, write Uncle Roberto. If Uncle Roberto cannot read English, ask your father to copy your letter in Italian. Here is a sample letter:

Dear Uncle Roberto,

I am starting to make a record of our family. My father says that you told him that your father was born November 3, 1902, in Italy. Is this date correct? Do you know where in Italy? Do you have any information about your grandparents? Any interesting facts about your parents' lives would help me. Thank you for your trouble.

Your Niece,

When grandma's sister became engaged, Uncle Roberto came from Italy for the occasion. What a feast the family had.

Uncle Roberto will probably be pleased with your interest. You can almost count on receiving the facts you mentioned. Store his letter in the manila envelope.

If your parents or grandparents have not been able to tell you the dates of some important events that happened to them in this country, you can get the information from a government office. Is it a birth or death date? You can write for these certificates. But you must know exactly where and when the events took place. Once you have that information, write the state, city or county department of records, asking how much the certificates will cost. If you want a marriage certificate, ask where you should write for that. Government offices may keep such certificates in different places.

Keep your letter simple, but include the following information:
1. The kind of certificate you want.
2. Full name of the person.
3. Exact date and place of the event, including the town, county and hospital, if you know it.
4. Sex of the person.
5. Money order or a certified check (which your parents can get for you), if you know the cost. If you don't, say that you will send a check or money order after they bill you.

By the way, never try to get a birth certificate for someone who is still living. That person should send for it. And, if you should happen to live in the city where the needed certificate is, an adult can go to the office and purchase it. See if you can go along, too.

If your grandparents came from another country and they are no longer living, don't give up! Ask one of your parents to write a relative or friend in that country, enclosing a pedigree chart, completed as far as possible. Even a distant cousin will be glad to fill in the blank spaces, if he or she can.

By now your notebook, tape recorder, and manila envelope may be crammed with information that you don't think you'll ever need. Don't worry about that. A true detective always collects more clues than are needed.

And don't throw anything away. Your grandparents may move away or may even die. Your own family may move, taking you far away from relatives who live around the corner now. Someday you might wish you could have another chance at that conversation, the way Alex Haley did.

One day your grandparents give you a box of snapshots. You weren't even alive when somebody with a Brownie box camera took pictures at a picnic. The pictures were carefully saved, although there are no names on the back. It didn't occur to anyone to write names there. Why should they? They all knew each other. Grandmother is sure that most of them must be family members or old friends. But she and

grandfather only recognize a few.

"Give me a chance to look at them a little longer," grandmother says. "I may figure out who is in some of the pictures. That could be my sister, Carol, in the big hat. Carol died 15 years ago."

Grandmother shows the picture to Aunt Carol's daughter, but she does not think the girl in the big hat is her mother. Do you think you would recognize a picture of your mother, taken when she was 17?

You are responsible for the photos you borrow. Since you will have to return them when you are finished, keep a record to whom they belong. Do not write on the backs of the picture, except with a special soft pencil called a China-Marker.

Now what's the next step? You still have a few blank spaces on your pedigree chart. You haven't been able to get enough information in order to write a four-generation history of your family. It is time to see your living great-grandparents. Or to write them if they live far away.

Unless a tape recorder bothers your great-grandparents, it will be even better to use when you talk to them. Probably because you don't know them quite as well as your grandparents.

You ask great-grandmother when her mother died.

"It was in the summer, just before the Fourth of July," she says. "I remember how strange it

When you find an excellent family group picture such as this, try to find somebody who can identify everyone.

seemed when our family didn't celebrate that year."

"What was the date?" you ask again.

"I thought I told you. It was July 2, 1897."

Your tape is filling up with wonderful stories, but it is hard to keep great-grandmother on the subject. You can see how much she likes talking about her childhood. Sometimes great-grandparents get so interested in talking about the past, they never do answer your questions.

If this should happen, ask your parents for help. They can probably get the answers you need.

When you write to great-grandparents who live far away, tell them what you are doing. Then enclose a short list of questions. Leave enough space after each one for the answer. As always, include a stamped, self-addressed envelope.

After the death of their great-grandfather, one family read his own account of his boyhood. Like so many people today, all they knew about life in the western United States seventy years ago came from television shows. Their great-grandfather's story showed them that tv shows aren't always right. And it was more interesting than tv, because it really happened to someone in their own family.

"Our breakfast consisted of either cornmeal or oatmeal mush or just plain rice, cooked. All we had on it was skim milk and a little sugar. Mother watched the sugar because you couldn't afford to have but a taste . . .

every speck of cream was made into butter, which we sold. Occasionally, we'd have what we called sowbelly—that was pork and it was home-cured and it was kind of hard to eat. We had dried apples and dried beans that we mixed in with corn beef or with our hams or bacon which we cured ourselves . . . It really wasn't too good," he wrote.

The children were especially interested when their great-grandfather described the unheated upstairs bedroom he slept in. His "mattress" was a piece of cloth, called a tick, filled with straw gathered from his father's fields. He had no blanket over him, winter or summer. He and his brothers had to sleep two to a bed "or we'd have frozen to death."

Completing Your Family History

At last, your pedigree chart is all filled up. How about the pictures and papers you had duplicated? This is the time you are going to use them. They will illustrate the family history you are about to write.

Empty your manila envelope on the kitchen table. Separate your notes into seven different piles, one for each of the couples on your pedigree chart.

Start with your parents. As a good detective, you had first questioned your parents. You have the dates and places they were born and married. You even have some pictures of them, so you can describe their looks and the clothes they wore. That's not enough. Write about their childhood and where they went to school. Tell where they met and were married.

Write about your father's occupation. Has he had a lot of different jobs? What were they? Tell about your mother's occupation. Does she have a paying job or does she work at home, taking care of your family? She isn't like any of your friends' mothers, is she? Why?

Do you have brothers and sisters? Tell about them.

After you have written the story of your own family, clip it to the family group sheet.

Any photos you cannot keep must now be returned. But you can make notes about things you saw in the photos you are returning. For instance, you saw an old car in one photo, and you found out it was a model from about 1955. That helped you to date the people in that photo.

Left: In 1922, grandfather was a baby.

Right: About the time your father was born in 1947, his grandparents bought this car.

Now, your grandparents. Your *maternal* grandfather (your mother's father) had served in the army in World War II. When he was discharged, he had years of schooling to make up. Possibly your grandmother received a degree, too, when he graduated. It was a fun degree, PHTC, which stands for "Putting Husband Through College." The degree was given to wives at many college graduations just after World War II. It meant that she had gotten a job, and the family lived on her earnings. There was one child—your mother. She was born when your grandfather was working hard to finish college.

Your *paternal* grandfather (your father's father) could have been in the air force or the navy during the war. Perhaps he was a paratrooper. Many soldiers died during that war, without ever seeing the children who were born while they were fighting. But

Notice how clothes change.

Left: Grandmother as a child, 1928.

Right: Mother as a child, 1959.

not in your paternal grandfather's case. He, too, went to college. He studied law and became a lawyer in the town in which he lived. Your father also became a lawyer and went to work in his father's company.

You have two family group sheets to attach to your grandparents' stories. Anything else you have about them—copies of pictures or originals, certificates—should be attached, too. Look closely at how they dressed in those days. Compare their clothes with the ones in your parents' photos. See the old trolley car in the background of one of them. There were very few buses then, and you got around the city by trolley. There aren't many trolley cars in the United States today.

Now the project is finished. You know more about yourself than you did before you went ancestor hunting. You have worked very hard finding your roots. It is a good feeling to know so much about yourself, isn't it?

Left: Great-grandfather in his World War I uniform.
Right: Grandfather in uniform, World War II.

Some Special Projects

All the information you have collected can be turned into a lovely family tree which you can hang on a wall, or give to someone as a gift. Here are three different ways you can make it.

Do you like to sew and embroider? Begin by drawing a tree with waterproof markers on a piece of white or light-colored sturdy cotton fabric. The tree should have eight branches, four on each side, with leaves on each branch. Draw fifteen circles hanging from the branches. Use a brown waterproof marker for the trunk and branches, a green one for the leaves, a red one to outline the circles, and black for the letters. Then embroider in those colors.

The circle at the top is for your name and birth date. The two circles on the next set of branches hold the names and birth dates of your parents. Farther down, the four circles are for your grandparents' names and birth dates. And the bottom eight circles hold your great-grandparents' names and dates.

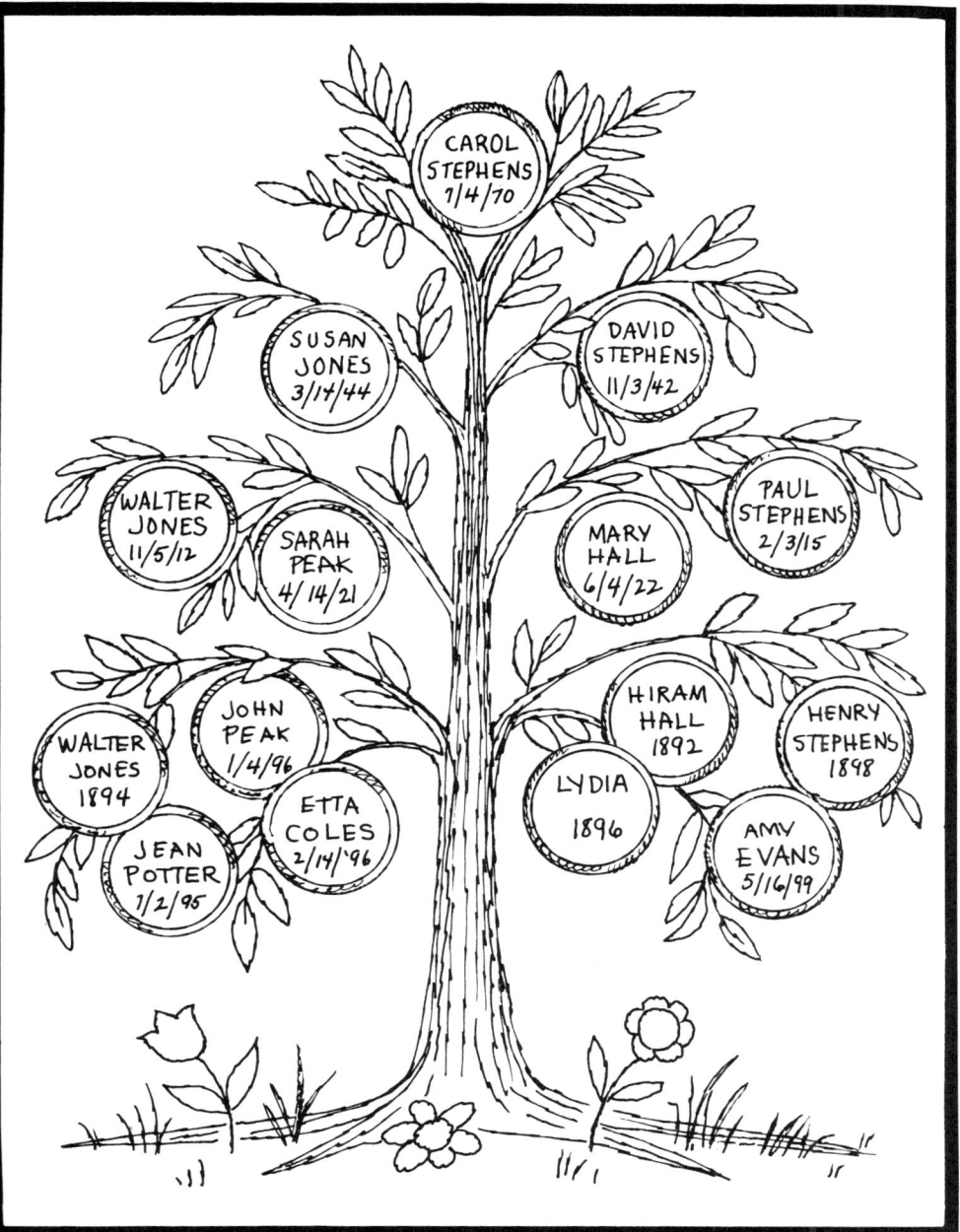

If you don't want to do any embroidery work, draw the same tree on a piece of poster paper with a magic marker. Then put small photographs in each of the circles. The name and birth date can be printed under each picture.

Maybe you don't have enough photographs to make a tree of pictures. In that case, draw a family tree but print the names and dates in the circles.

Re-read all those notes you've been taking. Isn't it surprising how many places your ancestors lived?

Buy an outline map of the United States, showing only state boundaries. Your teacher may have one to give you. If not, trace a map from an atlas. Then use a broken line to show how your family and ancestors moved all over the country, right up to today. Include such information as where they went to school, where they were married, where you and your brothers and sisters were born, and so forth.

Maybe you and your parents live in one state, say California. All of you have traveled throughout the state, and you have lived in one or two other California cities. You could always draw a map of your own state and trace the family moving through the state.

Perhaps you can get a map of the western hemisphere and show the birth places of all the ancestors on your pedigree chart. If they came from

FAMILY TRAVELS

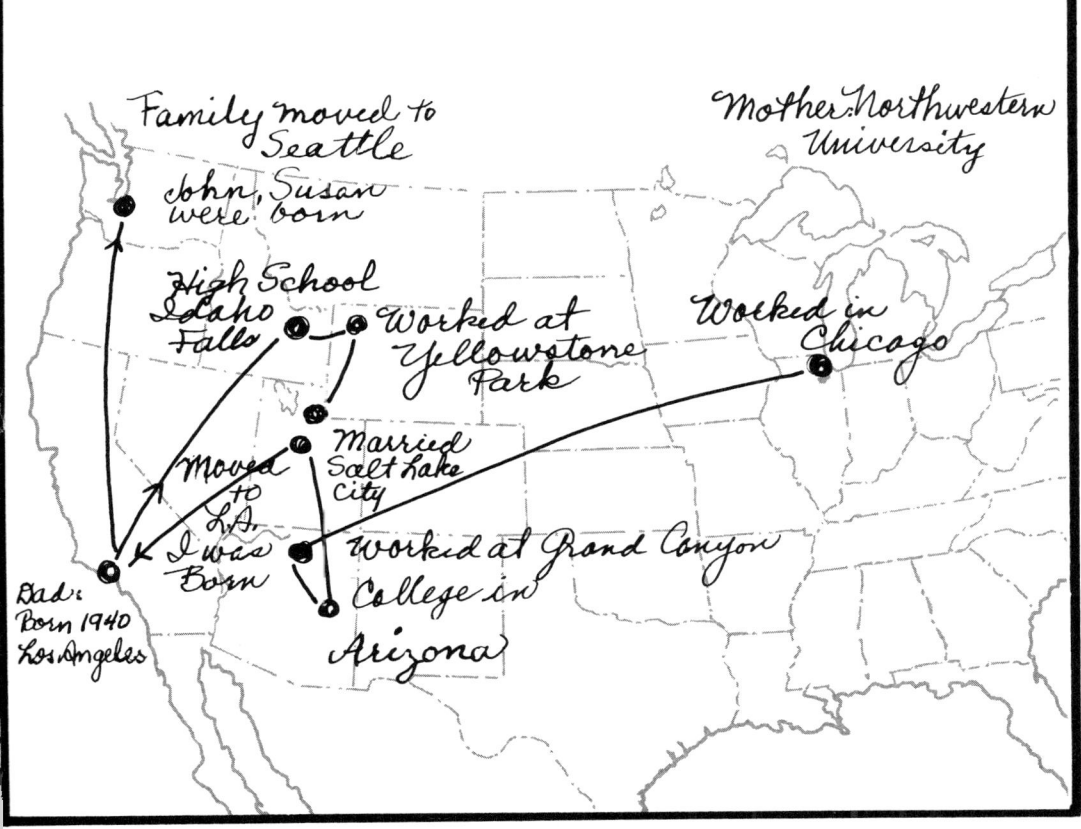

FAMILY BIRTHPLACES

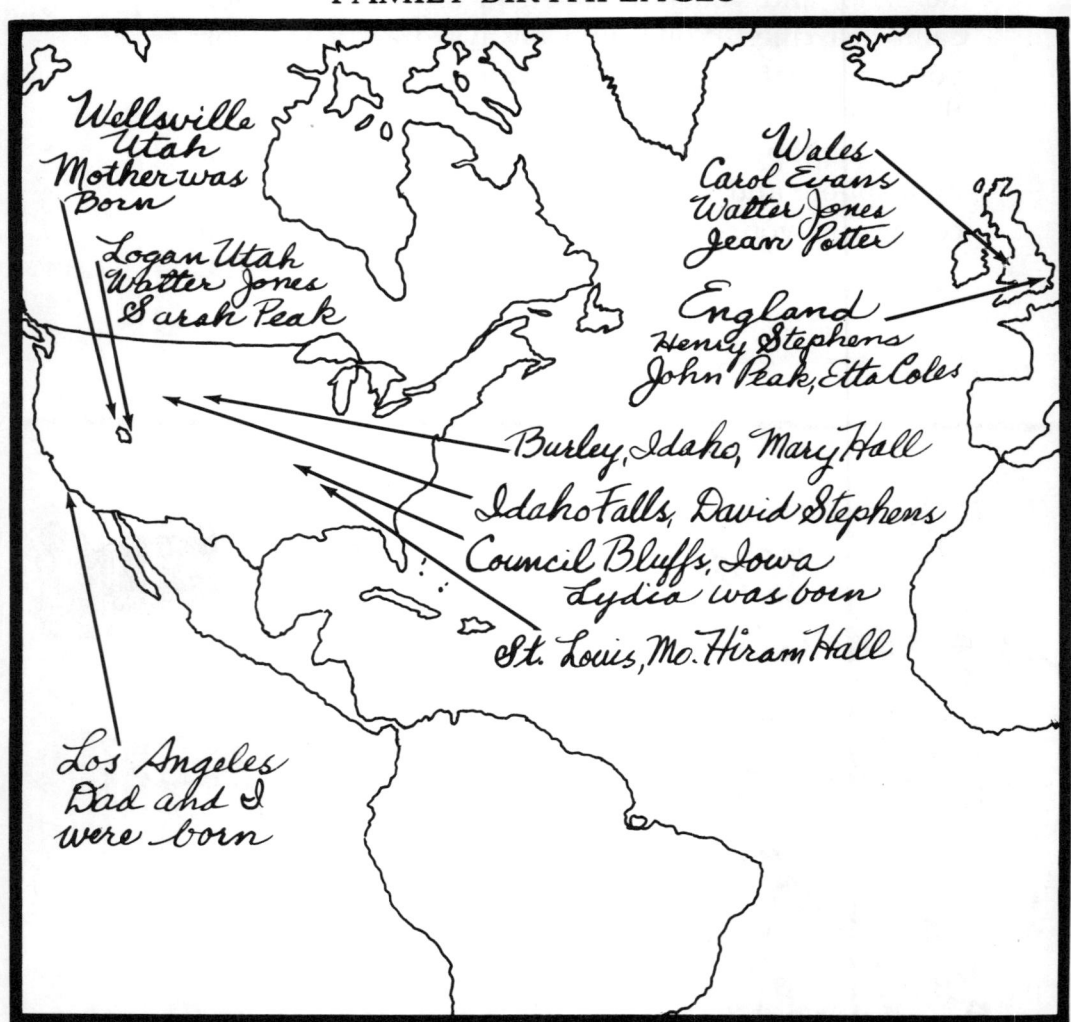

other parts of the world, draw maps of these places. Fill in the countries and the names of your ancestors.

Save up your money and have the maps and trees framed. Your bedroom walls will tell everyone about your new hobby.

Glossary

autobiography—the life story, written by the person who lived it.
biography—the life story of a person.
copyright—notice of ownership of a written or printed work.
descendants—the people who will come after you in your family.
diary—a personal record of day-to-day events which some people keep.
documenting—*See prove.*
environment—the place where you live and all the things around you.
genealogy—the tracing of your family from ancestors.
generation—all the people who were born at about the same time.
griot—an African word, used to mean a person who can recite the history of all the families in the village.
heraldry—the ancient custom of using special markings on shields to identify the family or rank of a person.
heredity—the passing of characteristics from generation to generation.
maternal—mother's side of the family.
Mayflower—the ship in which the Pilgrims sailed to America in 1620.
papyrus—an early kind of writing paper made from the papyrus plant.
parchment—an early kind of writing paper made from the skin of a sheep or goat.
paternal—father's side of the family.
pedigree—the line of ancestors of a person or an animal.
prove—to show that your information is true beyond any doubt. Sometimes it is called "documenting."
roots—your ancestors are your roots.

Index

A

ancestors, 7, 10, 18–22, 25, 34
autobiography, 24, 25

B

Bible, 43, 44
biography, 25
birth certificates, 32, 46, 47
Boy Scouts, 20

C

cemetery, 34–36
Church of Jesus Christ of Latter-day Saints (Mormon), 20, 21
copyright date, 43, 44

D

death certificates, 32, 46
detective, 10, 25
diary, 39
duplicating machine, 42

E

environment, 9

F

family group sheet, 28–30, 32, 40
family history, 29, 30
family tree, 56, 57, 61

G

genealogical libraries, 20
genealogy, 13, 16, 18
generation, 7, 8, 25
grandparents, 7, 8, 25, 32, 37–49
gravestones, 35, 36
great-grandparents, 8, 24, 25, 32, 37, 49–51

H

Haley, Alex, 19, 48
heraldry, 17
heredity, 8, 9
hobby, 11, 13, 18, 22

K

Kudrikas, Simas, 11, 12

L

letters, 45–47
life story, 22, 23

M

manila envelope, 11, 30–32, 52
map, 58–61
Mayflower, 18

N

notebook, 11, 30–32

O

opportunities, 9
oral tradition, 13

P

parents, 7, 24, 32, 52
pedigree chart, 25–27, 30–32, 40, 41, 49
pictures, 31, 53, 57

R

roots, 10, 19, 20

S

snapshots, 37, 39
scrapbooks, 37, 39

T

tape recorder, 38, 47, 49, 50